Written by
Don Walsh

Illustrated by
Lorraine Dey

Mill City Press
Minneapolis, MN

Mill City Press, Inc.
212 3rd Avenue North, Suite 290
Minneapolis, MN 55401
612.455.2294
www.millcitypublishing.com

ISBN-13: 978-1-62652-248-0

Printed in the United States of America

Teach the Beach

Chapter 1

As the school year came to an end, the Sands family began to make plans for their vacation at the beach. Their family consisted of the father, Sonny; the mother, Suzie; and their two children, Sean and Summer. The family had a pet hamster named Gidget. After a day of shopping to get all the supplies they would need for their vacation, Suzie returned in the family van to the small town where they lived, North Bay.

Making plans to be prepared in advance, Suzie said, "Sonny, be sure to have the van loaded tonight. I don't want to be late leaving in the morning, and please get the children to help you."

"I will," Sonny replied, thinking Suzie was being pesky for reminding him.

Early the next morning, to ensure her family was fed before getting on the road, Suzie woke the family and made them breakfast, so they wouldn't have to stop on the way to the beach.

Suzie said to the children, "Eat until you aren't hungry anymore; we aren't stopping to eat on the way to the beach."

Smiling, with a bite of pancake in her mouth, Summer said, "Sean, I'm so excited about going on vacation. I can hardly wait to get there!"

"Me, too!" Sean said, as he reached across the table for more orange juice.

"Okay, " Sonny said, "Let's get Gidget loaded in the van and get going."

"OH!" Summer exclaimed, "I need to go get Brownie Florence! She would be sad if I forgot her!" Brownie Florence, her favorite stuffed animal, went everywhere with Summer.

With Gidget and Brownie Florence safely loaded into the van, the Sands family headed for their summer vacation at Seaside Delight.

Chapter 2

Suzie looked out the van window as they arrived in town and said, "Seaside Delight is such a beautiful place!"

"Oh boy, I can't wait to get down to the beach!" Sean added.

"Not until we get the van unloaded!" Sonny grumbled. (Daddy was not so sunny when he was grumbly).

Mother added, "Help your father with the suitcases, children." (Mommy was always telling Summer and Sean what to do, and sometimes she was grumbly, too.)
The children worked quickly to get the van unloaded, so that they could go to the beach as soon as possible.

"Oh no, we forgot all about poor Gidget in the van!" Summer exclaimed.

Summer and Sean ran to get Gidget out of the van to bring her into the cottage.

"Okay, let's get changed into our bathing suits and go to the beach," said Sonny.

"It's about time!" Sean said to Summer.

"Yeah I thought we'd never get here!" Summer replied, grinning.

Everyone in the family went to their rooms, changed into their bathing suits, and headed for the beach. Walking onto the sand, the children headed straight for the ocean, while Sonny and Suzie set up the umbrella, beach chairs, blankets, and the cooler. Sean and Summer dropped their beach toys

as they ran toward the ocean.

"Hey, kids, what are you doing by the water without your parents?" a dolphin asked, popping his head up from the surf.

"Who are you?" Sean asked, with a surprised look on his face.

"I'm Donnie Dolphin and these are my friends: Aaron the seal, Ray the stingray, and Ringo Starfish. Who are you?" Donnie Dolphin replied.

"I'm Sean Sands, and this is my sister, Summer," Sean said.
"It's very nice to meet you," said Donnie, "Don't you know you should never be by the water without

your parents close by? You should always swim near a lifeguard!"

"There's the lifeguard over there!" Sean replied, pointing to the lifeguard stand in the center of the beach.

Aaron Seal added, "Yes, that's Justin Tyme. He's been on this beach longer than any other lifeguard."

"Well, it's very nice to meet all of you," Summer said, curling her toes in the sand.
"Me, too!" Sean added, picking up a seashell and skipping it across the water.

"Is this your first time at the beach?" Donnie asked.

"Yes," Sean replied.

Donnie thought for a moment and said, "Maybe we should go over some water safety tips, so you can enjoy your vacation."

Chapter 3

"Okay then, pay attention," Donnie said. "First of all, you should always swim near a lifeguard. Justin Tyme is the best lifeguard on the beach, and he will make sure you are safe."

"If you are going to be anywhere near the water or in the water, your parents should be there, too!" Aaron said. "Because the lifeguard can't watch everyone in the water at the same time."

Donnie added, "Your parents should be in the water with you, holding your hands."

"Thank you, I never knew that, Donnie and Aaron," Summer said.

"You may see flags flying on the beach," Donnie added. "A green flag means calm surf, and the water is safe for swimming. A yellow flag warns you to use caution and look around for danger—like big waves, or there might be a rip current that could pull you away from the beach. A blue flag means the area is reserved for boogie boards, rafts, and floats, or inflatable rafts or inner tubes. If you see a red flag, that means there is no swimming because the water is not safe!"

"Second, you should never dive into water you are not familiar with or have never been in before, because you could hit your head on the bottom of the ocean. This could happen if you dive in the water and don't know that the water is shallow or not very deep," Ray said, "You could hit a wooden piling from a wooden jetty or a rock."

"You should always walk into the water first before diving in to see how deep it is and what the bottom is like," Ringo said. "Besides, you could land on top of me!"

Donnie continued with the water safety tips. "Always look carefully at the ocean and have an idea of what the water is like before you go in. If it's high tide, the water will be deeper, and you may not be able to stand with your head above water."

"If its low tide, there may be waves. You'll want to be careful not to get caught in the waves if a set or group of them come crashing to shore," Aaron added.

Donnie added, "Waves sometimes come in 'sets' or groups, and you'll have to stand on the beach for a few minutes before entering the water just to see if there are any big waves coming in a set."

"You might not be able to catch your breath between the waves. It takes time to learn how to dive under them safely," Aaron added.

"Of course the more waves that come in a set, the deeper the water gets. You may not be able to stand up in the water any longer!" Ray said.

"If your feet can't touch the bottom, you may get pulled out to sea with the backwash," Ringo said.

"What's the backwash?" Sean asked.

"That's just the waves returning to the ocean. Some of you humans refer to it as the 'undertow,'" Ringo replied.

"Oh my! The ocean is starting to scare me," Summer exclaimed with alarm.

"Me, too!" added her brother.

"There's no need to be scared of the ocean, but you must learn to respect it," Donnie said, soothing the children.

"You must also learn how to handle yourself safely in the ocean," Aaron added. "Then you can truly enjoy your stay at the beach."

"Sean . . . Summer!" Sonny called.

The children heard their father call, "Come along with us. Your mother wants to go for a walk along the beach and collect some seashells."

"Sorry, guys, we have to go!" Sean said.

"Will all of you be here tomorrow?" Summer asked.

"We'll be here tomorrow," Donnie replied.

"We're here every day," Aaron added.

"Goodbye!" Sean said.

"It was very nice to meet all of you," Summer added.

"It was very nice meeting you and your brother," Aaron said.

"Mom! Wait until you hear about our new friends!" Summer said excitedly as she ran to her mother.

"They're the best!" Sean added.

"We met a dolphin named Donnie, a seal named Aaron, a stingray named Ray, and Ringo Starfish!" Summer explained happily. "They were starting to teach Sean and me how to be safe in the ocean."

"Then we heard you call us to go look for seashells," Sean added. "We wanted to stay by the water and learn more from our new friends."

"You'll be able to see a lot more of your new friends, don't worry. This is just the first day of our vacation," Dad said, as Sean and Summer started down the beach on their search for seashells.

Chapter 4

The next day, the children returned to the beach and looked for their friends, but they were nowhere to be found.

"Do you think it's okay to go in the water and look for our new friends: Donnie, Aaron, Ray, and Ringo Starfish?" Sean asked.

"No, remember what they told us yesterday? We should never go in the water unless our parents are here to watch us," Summer replied.

"Well, I don't see any waves; and Justin Tyme is right over there to watch us, so I'm going in," Sean said.

"I don't think we should be doing this," Summer said.

"How do you expect to find our friends in the ocean unless we go in?" Sean asked.

"I guess you're right," Summer replied.

"Let's start looking over here by the rock jetty," Sean said.

The two ventured into the water alongside the rock jetty to look for their friends. Before long, they were being pulled out to sea by a rip current, which is water running out to sea away from the beach.

"Oh no!" Summer cried out.

"Start swimming for shore!" Sean shouted.

"I feel like my body is being pulled out into the ocean away from the shore!" Summer cried.

"Swim harder!" Sean said.

"I can't!" Summer shouted, "The ocean is too strong for me!"

The children swam as hard as they could, but the rip current kept taking them farther away from shore. As the current took the children out along the rock jetty, the water rushed faster and faster out to sea. Just as the two children thought they weren't going to make it back to shore, their new friends from the ocean surfaced to rescue them.

At that moment, Justin Tyme leaped from his lifeguard stand with his torpedo rescue floatation device in hand and raced toward the children.

"Sean, hold onto me, and I'll pull you to safety!" Donnie shouted.

Aaron added, "Summer, hold onto me and I'll pull you away from the rocks."

"You should never try to fight the rip current, it's too strong!" Donnie told them. "Always swim parallel, or the same way the waves are coming to shore, to get out of a rip current."

"Other ways to escape a rip current are doggie paddle to the side or Flip, Float, and Follow" "Flip onto your back, Float and Follow the rip current out past the waves out of danger," added Aaron.

"We're headed out past the waves, and we'll wait there for Justin Tyme," Donnie said. "Justin Tyme will bring you back to the beach safely."

Justin Tyme swam out to where Donnie and Aaron were, and safely pulled the children using his torpedo to help them float. He brought them back to the beach.

"What causes a rip current?" Summer asked, back on the beach.

"Usually the cause is wind blowing toward a rock jetty or wooden jetty, pushing the surface water toward the rocks. When the water gets next to the rocks, it has no place to go but to rush out to sea," Donnie explained.

"You can usually tell there is a rip current because the water will be a different color, lighter than the rest of the ocean, and you'll learn to avoid those dangerous areas," Aaron added.

Sean and Summer called out, "Thank you!" to Donnie, Aaron, and Ray.

"And thank you, Justin Tyme!" Summer said, "You're the best!"

The children, who were soaking wet, returned to their summer cottage, "Wit's End," to tell their parents what happened, and how they were rescued by their new friends.

"I think I've had enough of the ocean for today," Summer said.

Suzie said, "Let's all take a walk to the inlet and watch the boats. We can have an early lunch there, and the walk will do us good." Suzie dried Summer and Sean with towels, and they followed their mother and father out the door for a walk.

The family walked to the inlet and enjoyed hot dogs, sodas, and ice cream at Keith's Korner while watching the boats go in and out of the inlet. They returned home, walking along the water's edge, gathering seashells, and spending the rest of the day together. The children were tired from their ocean adventure, but by this time they were feeling a lot better.

Chapter 5

The next morning, Sean and Summer were up early and couldn't wait to get back to the beach, so they left Wit's End cottage before their parents were awake. They were excited about seeing their friends again.

"Uh oh, I don't see any of our ocean friends," Sean said.

"Me neither," Summer replied. "You're not going in the water to look for them, are you?"

Sean asked her, "How are we going to find them standing on the beach?"

"Maybe they'll just show up," Summer answered.

"I don't think so," Sean said doubtfully. "We'll just go into the water in the center of the beach, away from the rocks, and we'll be fine. Besides, Justin Tyme is on duty, and he'll watch out for us."

Just as they had done the day before, Summer and Sean waded into the water to look for their friends, completely unaware of the danger waiting for them.

Summer shouted, "Sean, I think that we are headed for the rock jetty again!"

"No, we're fine," Sean replied calmly. "We've got plenty of room."

"I don't think so!" Summer exclaimed!

"Oh no, I think you're right!" cried Sean.

"HELP! HELP! HELP!" Summer screamed. "I can't swim to shore!"

"Oh no!" Ringo called out to his briny friends. "Ray, wake up and go find Donnie and Aaron; the kids are in trouble!"

Ray flew upward and rushed off to find Donnie and Aaron. After finding Donnie and Aaron, they all rushed off to go rescue the children. Justin Tyme heard Summer cry for help, and he took off down the beach to rescue the children.

Once again Donnie, Aaron, and Ray pulled the children out of danger and waited for Justin Tyme to arrive with his torpedo.

Justin arrived and the children thanked Donnie, Aaron, and Ray for helping them to safety, just as they had the day before.

"Where are your parents?" Justin asked.

"They're at home," Sean replied shyly.

"You should never go swimming without you parents!" Justin scolded them.

"We know," Summer replied ashamed, "Don't we!" With that, Summer nudged Sean with her arm.

"You're right," Sean replied reluctantly. "I'm sorry."

Once they were safely ashore, Justin Tyme sat them down on the sand and went back to his lifeguard stand. When their ocean friends reappeared, Summer asked them, "Why were we being pulled toward the rock jetty?"

"You were caught in a sweep," Donnie explained.

"What's a sweep?" Sean asked.

"The wind can move the surface water along the beach, and it will take you along with it," Donnie explained. "Even though the wind stopped blowing overnight, the water was still moving along the

beach and you couldn't see it."

"That was scary," Summer said, shaking.

"You should always have a reference point picked out before you go in the water," Aaron added.

Sean asked, "What's a reference point?"

"You should find a house on the beachfront or use the lifeguard stand as a reference point and stay in front of the house or lifeguard stand when you are in the water," Aaron answered him. "Make sure you stay in front of that reference point while you swim."

"That way if there is a current pulling you down the beach, you'll know it right away; and you'll have more time to get to safety," Ray added. "Now you had better get back to your parents before they start to worry!"

"You're right, we'd better go," Summer said.

Sean grabbed his sister's hand, as they started back toward their cottage, they called out, "See you tomorrow!"

Donnie, Aaron, and Ray watched as Sean and Summer walked up the beach, shaking their heads and smiling. Once the children were out of sight, the sea creatures swam out beyond the sand bar to play in the waves.

Chapter 6

The next day, the children waited for their parents to get up, and the family went to the beach together. They didn't bother to tell their parents that they had to be saved from a possible drowning a second time. At the beach, Sean and Summer helped their parents set up the umbrella, chairs, blankets, cooler, and beach toys. When everything was ready, the family decided to go for a swim together.

As they walked down to the shoreline, Sean said to his parents, "We should stand on the beach and watch to see if there are any big waves coming before we go in the ocean."

"We also need to see if there are any rip currents by checking for water that is a different color than the rest," added his sister.

Suzie looked at them with surprise; her mouth dropped open, and she said, "I'm impressed! Where did you learn all of this?"

"We learned it from our new friends," Summer answered.

"They're teaching us how to be safe in the ocean," Sean added.

Suzie was pleased when she heard the warnings her children were reciting. "That's so good to hear," Suzie said. "I feel a lot better about letting you kids go in the water now."

"Come on, let's go!" Sean yelled.

Sonny pointed down the shoreline to a specific area of the beach. "Let's go in over there. I don't see any waves breaking, and it looks safe."

The family waded into the ocean in an area where they thought it was safe. There were waves breaking on either side of them, but no waves were breaking in the area where they wanted to go swimming. They entered the water between two sand bars where the water was deeper. They were unaware at the time that the real reason there were no waves breaking is that water always seeks its own level. The water from the sand bars on each side of them was collecting in the middle, forming a rip current and rushing back out to sea. The Sands family was heading right into a rip current, and they did not realize it!

"Oh no!" Summer shrieked, "I think we are being pulled out to sea!"

"Grab the children!" Sonny yelled to Suzie. "Try and hold on, Summer!"

"I can't!" Summer shouted back.

"We're going out to sea!" Sean cried.

"I can't believe it!" Summer shouted. "What's happening now?"

"Ray, the Sands family is in trouble!" Ringo called out to his ocean friends. "Go get Donnie and

Aaron!" Ray quickly arrived on the scene with Donnie and Aaron and was surprised to see the whole family in danger. Justin Tyme blew his whistle to get help from the other lifeguards on duty. Donnie, Aaron, and Ray managed to pull the Sands family out of danger and waited for Justin Tyme and his lifeguard pals to arrive.

After Donnie, Aaron, and Ray pulled the Sands family out of danger, looking at the ocean creatures gratefully, Sonny said, "Thank you for helping us."

"So, you must be Sean and Summer's new friends," Suzie added, as she treaded water.

"Yes, I'm Donnie and this is Aaron, Ray, and Ringo Starfish," Donnie explained, introducing his friends.

"This is certainly an odd time to introduce myself, but my name is Sonny Sands and it's very nice to meet you," Sonny said, as he held onto Aaron .

"Yes, and I'm Suzie Sands, and we are very grateful for your help," Suzie added.

A few moments later, Justin Tyme and his pals arrived to accompany the Sands family safely back to the beach.

Once they were all safely on the sand, Sonny stood on the beach and said, "Thank you so much for saving my family!" as he shook Justin Tyme's hand.

A teary-eyed Suzie said, "Yes, thank all of you for saving us."

Looking at his wet and scared children, Sonny said, "I think that was enough excitement for one day."

Nodding her head, Suzie said, "I agree!"

"Let's go sit down and relax on our blanket for a while," Suzie suggested.

"Can we go for a walk later and collect some more seashells, Mom, please?" Summer asked.

"Yes, you can," Suzie answered. "That sounds like it will be a lot safer than going back in the water!"

Chapter 7

The next day, the Sands returned to the beach as a family. Sonny refused to allow his children to go to the beach alone.

"Can we please go in the water, Dad?" Sean pleaded.

Sonny studied the ocean for a few minutes and said, "No, the waves are too big! It doesn't look safe."

"Will you go with us to the edge of the water while we wait for our friends?" Sean asked.

"Okay" Sonny replied, "But only at the water's edge, and not any deeper than your knees."

"Let's go!" Summer shouted. "I feel safer having you go in the water with us, Daddy."

The family walked to the edge of the water and stood knee deep in the ocean, holding hands with one another.

"Wow, those waves out there are really big!" Sean exclaimed. "Look! It's Donnie, Aaron, and Ray riding the big waves!"

"They make it look easy, don't they?" added Summer.

Concerned, Suzie asked, "Are you sure we're safe here, Sonny?"

"We'll be fine," Sonny replied. "Just don't let go of my hand."

Just then, a set of big waves came in and roared up to the beach.

"Oh no!" Summer cried out in alarm. "I can't touch the bottom anymore! The water's too deep!"

"Hold onto the children!" Sonny yelled, as the backwash (or "undertow") took the family away from the beach.

"Ringo Starfish, always on the alert for danger, saw that the family was in trouble again.

Ringo called out to his ocean friends, "Donnie! Aaron! Ray! The Sands are in trouble and need our help now!"

"HELP! HELP! HELP!" Sonny cried out.

Justin Tyme heard the cries for help, grabbed his torpedo, and jumped from his lifeguard stand, running down the beach toward where he heard the cries for help. His lifeguard pals were busy saving others at that exact moment, so he was on his own. Just as the Sands family found themselves being pulled out further into the ocean waves, Donnie, Aaron, and Ray arrived to rescue them.

Donnie shouted, "Mr. and Mrs. Sands, grab onto my fin, and I'll pull you out past the waves."

Aaron instructed the children, "Sean and Summer, hold onto Ray and me, and we'll swim you clear of the waves."

Justin Tyme jumped into the water and started swimming out through the big surf toward the Sands, while Donnie, Aaron, and Ray made sure that the family was pulled safely from the waves.

Sean shouted excitedly, "Here comes Justin Tyme!"

Swimming up to the family, Justin said, "I saw you get hit by the big waves, and I knew you didn't stand a chance of swimming out of danger on your own. Hold onto my torpedo, and I'll swim you to shore as soon as we get a break in the waves."

Even though the family was safely pulled to shore, their ocean friends stayed close. Suzie asked them, "How did that happen?"

"Your whole family was pulled out by the backwash that was created by the big waves," Donnie replied.

"But we were standing in knee-deep water!" Sonny asserted.

"Even though you were in the shallow water, when a big set of waves hit the beach, the water becomes deep instantly, and you can no longer hold your footing," Aaron explained.

"I guess we still have so much to learn about the ocean. Thank you again," Suzie said, still shaking from the ordeal.

"Thanks for your help, Donnie, Aaron, Ray, and Ringo!" Sonny added.

The Sands family all thanked Justin Tyme as well for coming to their rescue.

"Thank you, Justin!" the Sands family said together.

Exhausted from the day's frightening turn of events, Suzie said, "If this keeps up, we'll have to limit our activity to collecting seashells, walks to the inlet to watch the boats, and sunbathing on the beach."

Summer thought about what her mother said and replied, "No, Mommy! Aaron told us that we have to learn how to handle ourselves in the ocean."

Sean added, "And Donnie told us we had to learn how to respect the ocean! Once we learn how to respect the ocean, we can enjoy swimming in the ocean safely."

The family returned to their blankets and relaxed for the rest of the day under the heat of the warm summer sun.

Chapter 8

The next morning, the Sands family returned to the beach to see what new adventures awaited them.

"It certainly was windy last night," Suzie commented.

Sonny agreed; "I know, it was a very strong northeast wind."

The Sands arrived on the beach and set up their blankets in the usual manner. Sean was the first to check out the ocean.

"WOW! Look at all those rip currents!" Sean cried.

"I wonder what caused so many rip currents to appear?" Summer asked.

Sean cried out, "Look! There's Donnie, Aaron, and Ray riding the waves!"

"Can we go ask our ocean friends what caused all the rip currents, Dad?" asked Summer.

"Yes," replied Sonny. "But only if you don't go in the water and stay on the beach at the shoreline."

Suzie added, "Listen to your father, children!"

"We will!" both children shouted together as they ran toward the edge of the beach.

The children ran down to the edge of the water and called to their friends Donnie, Aaron, and Ray.

Aaron happened to be near the shoreline; and when he heard the children, he called out, "Hi, kids!"

"You two better not try any swimming today; it's too rough," Donnie said.

"We know, but what's causing all the rip currents?" Summer inquired.

"The northeast wind last night eroded the beach. Now the water's edge is cupped, or scalloped, as a result," Donnie explained. "As the waves return to the ocean from the beach, the water collects at the lowest point and rushes back out to sea, forming rip currents."

Ray asked, "By now, the two of you have learned to avoid the lighter colored water of the rip currents, haven't you?"

Sean and Summer replied in unison, "We certainly have!"
"I guess it's a good day for a walk to the inlet to watch the boats," Sean said.

Summer agreed, saying, "Let's go get Mom and Dad."

"Okay," Sean said, a bit reluctantly.

"Goodbye, Donnie. Goodbye Aaron, and goodbye Ray," the children said sadly.

"Goodbye," Donnie, Aaron, and Ray replied.

"They sure are nice," Summer remarked, as they walked up the beach to their blanket.

"Mom, Dad, it's too rough to go in the ocean today!" Sean said. "Let's take a walk to inlet and watch the boats."

"That's a good idea," Sonny replied with a smile, realizing that his children had learned some important water safety tips.

Chapter 9

The next day, the Sands family returned to the beach, but this time there wasn't a wave in sight, and the ocean was as flat as a pancake. The wind had switched direction overnight. Now it was coming from the land, and all the waves were flat.

Surveying the scene, Sean turned to his father and said, "The ocean looks like a lake today, Dad."

"It certainly does," his father replied.

Suzie looked at the ocean and then at her husband and said, "I guess it's safe to let the children go in today."

Summer pleaded, "Can we take our tubes in today, Dad?"

"Yes," Sonny replied. "Your mother and I will sit at the water's edge and keep any eye on you both."

The children sat in their tubes and paddled away from the beach. Sean began to playfully tease his sister by trying to pull Summer out of her tube. By using his legs, Sean succeeded in pulling Summer right out of her tube into the water.

"Sean that wasn't very nice!" Summer yelled at her brother.

"I was just fooling around!" Sean said with a grin. "I didn't mean anything by it," he added innocently.

After a short while, the west wind began to blow Summer's tube out to sea and beyond her reach.

"Sean, I can't get to my tube!" Summer cried.

"I'll get it for you!" Sean shouted as he jumped out of his tube to swim after his sister's tube.

Ringo, always watching out for the children's safety, was observing Sean and Summer playing in the water. Turning to his ocean friend, he asked, "Do you see what's going on over there, Ray?"

"They'll never catch those tubes in a west wind!" Ray replied, "I'm on my way to get Donnie and Aaron."

Sonny called out for help to Justin Tyme to get his attention on the lifeguard stand, but he had already seen what had happened and was on his way to the rescue.

"Sean!" cried Donnie. "Don't even try swimming out to retrieve that tube! You'll never catch the tube with this west wind!" "Sean and Summer, grab onto my fin and I'll pull you to shore!"

"I'll get your tubes for you, don't worry!" Aaron said as he quickly zipped across the water to rescue the tubes for Sean and Summer.

Aaron easily caught the tubes and returned them to the beach for the children. Meanwhile, Donnie swam the children back.

"Yeah, it seems like you're always there when we need you. Thanks!" Sean added, feeling foolish for his prank.

"It's our pleasure," Donnie replied.

"We just want to be sure that you enjoy your stay at Seaside Delight," Aaron added, "and to be certain that you are safe while you are here. Don't forget to thank Ray and Ringo!"

"Oh, sorry! We didn't mean to leave you out! Thank you, Ray and Ringo!" Summer said, "You guys are the greatest!"

"Same goes for me!" added Sean, "You guys are the best!"

"And thanks again to you, Justin. You are the best lifeguard on the beach!" Summer said.

Justin replied modestly, "That's very kind of you to say. It's nice to know that I'm appreciated."

Hugging her children, Suzie said gratefully, "You are appreciated; believe me, you are!"

Sonny, standing next to his wet brood, added, "That goes double for me!"

The Sands returned to their blankets to dry off the children and relax. Sonny told Sean and Summer that they were lucky to have friends like Donnie, Aaron, Ray, Ringo, and Justin Tyme. The children agreed and were very grateful to have a group of guardian angels on land and in the ocean, watching over them.

Chapter 10

Returning from their favorite lunch spot at the inlet, the family walked by the water's edge and watched Donnie, Aaron, and Ray playing in the shallow water.

"Hey, kids" Donnie called, "Why don't you come in the water and join us?"

"That's a great idea!" added Aaron, "I'll show you how I dive off Ray's back. It's lots of fun!"

The Sands family waited a while to give their lunch time to digest, which is always best. If you do go swimming after you eat, and get a cramp in your stomach, that doesn't mean that your arms and legs don't work. You're still able to swim.

Summer turned to her father and asked, "Can we go in, Daddy?"

"Certainly, the wind has died down, and you'll be with your friends; so, go ahead" Sonny said.

As the children scrambled into the water, Summer turned around with a grin and said, "Thanks, Dad!"

"Oh no!" Sean yelped as he entered the water.

"What's wrong?" Sonny asked, alarmed at the prospect of another potential danger.

Looking scared, Sean shouted to his parents on shore; "The water's warm! That means there will be sharks around today!"

"Now what makes you think that?" Donnie commented. "People swim in the ocean when the water is warm, but the sharks live in the ocean all the time! What happens when the water gets cold? . . . Where would the sharks go to live?

"No need to worry, we haven't seen any sharks around here in years," added Aaron.

Guessing that the ocean animals knew about sharks better than humans, Suzie relaxed and shouted to Donnie and Aaron from the beach, "Thank you! I feel much better now."

Ray chimed in, "Come on, let's play kids; there's nothing to worry about! Hurry up before I'm due for my nap!"

Watching his children frolicking in the water, Sonny said, "Now this is more like it. It's great to see our children enjoying the ocean, and it's nice that their friends are there to watch over them."

Smiling as she watched Sean and Summer, Suzie hugged her husband happily, saying, "I agree."

Chapter 11

With the end of the Sands' vacation drawing near, the family made an effort to spend as much time as possible on the beach, enjoying the ocean, and walking along the beach collecting shells. One afternoon, while the family walked along the ocean, Sean noticed another brother and sister playing in the water by themselves, no parents in sight, at the water's edge.

"I should tell those children that they should only be swimming in the water when their parents are close by, watching them," said Sean.

Admiring Sean's thoughtfulness, Sonny said, "Why don't you do that, Sean. That's a good idea."

The family stopped walking and Sean called out to the brother and sister.

Sean shouted, "Hey, kids, you shouldn't be swimming unless your parents are sitting nearby, watching you when you're in the water!"

Summer wanted to help make the point so she added in a loud voice, "Yeah! And you should always swim in front of a lifeguard!"

With that, the children returned to shore and thanked Sean and Summer.

Smiling, the young girl walked up to Sean and Summer and said, "We never thought about having someone watch us when we are in the water. I guess we should go get our parents and swim in front of a lifeguard. "Thanks for the good advice."

The Sands family continued walking down the beach. As they approached a rock jetty, they spotted three young boys swimming and ducking in and out of the waves very close to the rocks. Sean pointed out to his parents that the boys were headed for trouble since they were so close to the rocks with waves approaching. Sonny said, "I think you had better warn them, too."

Sean called out to the boys in the water, "Hey, you guys, it's not safe to swim so close to the rocks with the waves coming in like that! Swim parallel or along the beach until you're away from the rock jetty."

"Remember to always swim in front of a lifeguard." Summer added.

The group of boys replied, "Good idea and thanks!" They swam safely away from the rock jetty, stopping in front of the lifeguard stand where Justin Tyme could keep a close eye on them.

Smiling as she watched the boys follow Sean and Summer's suggestions, Suzie said, "It looks like we have a couple of junior lifeguards in the making, Sonny!"

Sonny chuckled, "Yes, It's also nice to know that they both have learned their lessons on how to be safe in the ocean, and to see that they are concerned about the safety of others."

Suzie agreed, "We've got a lot to be proud of where our children are concerned!"

"Maybe someday in the future, we'll see Sean and Summer up on the lifeguard stand, just like Justin Tyme," Sonny added.

"That would be fun if we could help other people!" Sean said excitedly.

"Yeah, I'd like that, too," Summer added as she kicked sand between her toes.

Chapter 12

The family reached the end of the beach and headed back toward their blanket. They thought about the end of their vacation, and returning to Seaside Delight the following year.

"Mom and Dad, can we come back to Seaside Delight next year? Pleeeease!" Summer pleaded.

Suzie added, "Yes, I think we should, and I'd like to stay in that lovely little cottage 'Wit's End' again."

Thinking about the prospect, Sonny added cautiously, "That's if our grumpy old landlord, Mr. Crabcake lets us. I'll try to convince him."

"I know the children would be a lot safer swimming here at Seaside Delight, knowing that they would have their friends to watch over them," Suzie added.

Looking thoughtful, Summer said, "We've made some very special friends here, and we have a lot to be thankful for."

Sonny, Suzie, and Sean chimed in together, "We agree!"

Looking out into the ocean, the Sands family cheered happily as they watched Donnie, Aaron, Ray, and Ringo playing in the ocean. Even Justin Tyme, the lifeguard, stood up and cheered!

Summer called out to her ocean friends, "You guys are the greatest! What a great way to end our vacation!"

Dedicated to the memory of Aaron Carson Vaughn

Elite Navy SEAL, Aaron Carson Vaughn, was killed August 6, 2011, when a Chinook chopper carrying thirty American troops was shot down in Afghanistan. Aaron had just celebrated his thirtieth birthday.

After serving in SEAL Team One for many years, Special Operations Chief Vaughn, in May of 2010, began rigorous selection and training with Naval Special Warfare Development Group . He endured several months of the most rigorous training offered in the military, and upon successful completion reported to Development and Evaluation Squadron Three in December 2010. Aaron completed numerous deployments around the world, including several combat deployments to Afghanistan and Iraq.

He was a highly decorated combat veteran with numerous awards, including the Joint Service Achievement Medal with Valor, Navy and Marine Corps Achievement Medal with Valor, Combat Action Ribbon, Good Conduct Medal, Iraq Campaign Medal, Afghanistan Campaign Medal, Global

War on Terrorism (Service) Medal, Global War on Terrorism (Expeditionary) Medal, and numerous other personal and unit decorations. He was posthumously awarded the Purple Heart, the Defense Meritorious Service Medal, and the Bronze Star Medal with Valor.

On the personal side . . .

Aaron gave his life to Christ at a very early age and, because of that, he had a discernment that was uncharacteristic of a young boy, including a keen ability to see this world in black and white. He was never afraid to recognize or call out evil. By the time he was eight years old, he began telling anyone who would listen, "One day I'm going to be a Navy SEAL." He overcame unimaginable odds to achieve that dream.

Growing up on a small farm in West Tennessee, he loved fishing, hunting, football, 4-wheeling, mudding, and, later, after moving to Florida, surfing. But most of all . . . he loved his God, his family, and his country. Aaron never took for granted the fact that he had been blessed enough to have been born in the United States of America, the land of the free.

May his legacy live on through the lives of his children and all those who knew and loved him.

GOD BLESS AMERICA

Aaron and his wife, Kimberly Vaughn

I would like to thank my wife, Millie, and my son, Sean, for all their love and support during the evolution of this project. There are so many that have helped to bring my book to life, and I'm very grateful for their input and support. I especially thank Nancy Steadman-Martin for her advice along the way.

Don Walsh, Author

I grew up on the Jersey shore and, as a child, you couldn't keep me out of the water. And you still can't! I've been swimming in the ocean every month for the past 144 months in a row for a total of twelve years. At the age of seventeen, I became an ocean lifeguard with numerous rescues to my credit over the years. An avid open water swimmer, I've been competing in ocean races for over three decades in distances from one mile up to 6.2 miles (10K). I have also completed the 12.5 mile swim around Key West, a 21-mile swim down the Mays Landing River in New Jersey, twice completed the 28.5-mile Manhattan Swim Marathon, and in 2006, I became the first person from New Jersey to swim around the Isle of Jersey located in the English Channel—a distance of 41.5 miles. I have coached at the club, high school, and college levels, in addition to spending six years traveling across the country, coaching triathletes. I coach a triathlon team out of Chicago, "Team Dream," and we're starting a New York Chapter. For the past fourteen years, I've been mentoring Special Warfare candidates for the Navy teaching Combat Side Stroke.

I also have a DVD produced by GOSWIM.TV "Combat Side Stroke with Don Walsh."

My book is intended to provide guidelines so that families may enjoy the ocean safely. If my book saves the life of one child, it's worth everything.

Lorraine Dey, Illustrator

"I have lived along the Jersey shore since I was fifteen. So much of my life includes memories of enjoying the ocean and beaches of this area. I was excited to join forces with Don to help him bring this important information to families who visit the shore and may not be aware of the ocean's changing tides and currents. Don explains, in simple terms, what to look for in order to be safe while swimming at the shore."

Lorraine Dey has been a full-time illustrator and graphic designer for over thirty years. Lorraine began drawing as soon as she could pick up a crayon, and she would spend hours drawing and coloring as a little girl. "Lorrie," as she is known to her friends and family, lives at the Jersey shore with her two cats, Jodie and Mischief.

She has illustrated *A Sweater for Duncan,* and also written and illustrated *The Rain Forest Party,* two children's picture books published by Raven Tree Press.